Stop Your Divorce and Save Your Marriage!

TABLE OF CONTENTS

Introduction

If you saw the emotional turmoil portrayed in the movies War of the Roses and Kramer vs. Kramer, you'd probably think twice about divorce. Unhappy individuals who believe that ending their marriage would make them happier are often living a myth.

Chances are that they've attributed the failure of the marriage to their spouse, dispensing with self-examination. Blaming the other instead of oneself becomes the favorite pastime, the most convenient means to walk away.

By failing to accept their own frailties, and not realizing that they've entered the marriage with unreasonable demands and unrealistic expectations, they unconsciously released the forces leading to a potential separation.

There's also the phenomenon of short memories. For some reason, the same individuals who vowed to support each other during their time of wedded bliss have forgotten their commitment and vows to love each other through thick and thin.

Our modern society has indeed become a disposable society. This is what Alvin Toffler had predicted almost two decades ago. This state of "disposableness" is reflected in our ability to DELETE and PURGE and SHRED what we no longer need.

And when our once beloved partner is no longer of use to us, we call our lawyer and instruct him/her to initiate divorce proceedings.

Funny, but despite its harrowing and complex web, divorce has also become just a phone call away, a "to go" solution that we can pick up on the way to cleaner's.

Truth is, is that divorce has an *ugly side to it*. It's the easy way out for people who have not an ounce of courage to salvage what deserves to be salvaged.

Divorce *un-builds* and *undoes* what took years to nurture, and sadly, often the only people who benefit from it are greedy lawyers who will use every trick in the book to divest the other of assets, until no remnant of the person's investment – physical, monetary and emotional – remains.

While divorcing couples spend their mental energies accusing the other of causing hurt and disharmony in the union, they forget that the children suffer in double – triple dosages. Couples forget that the sentiments of children are more fragile and harder to mend. This is when the concept of human selfishness and self-centredness become transparent. It's odd how the true character of people comes out when they're the actors in a divorce.

The determination not to be swayed by the lows and downs of a relationship mirrors strength and integrity, not to mention the ability to see beyond one's personal unhappiness. And by saving the marriage, more than one human being is saved.

This is the essence of this ebook in your hands right now; perhaps the most important that you'll ever read.

The Unpleasant Side of Divorce

Getting married is entering into a contract - but it's probably the one contract that is the easiest to break because divorce has made it easy for husband and wife to walk out when they go through an unhappy period in their life, albeit temporary.

John Crouch, Executive Director of Americans for Divorce Reform, says that the most important economic contract of our lives – marriage – is no longer legally protected.

Just think – lawyers will fight *tooth and nail* to protect corporations in their contract relations or between you and your landlord, your mechanic and your doctor, but can't prevent you from breaking up with your spouse. In fact, they would even counsel you to break up your marriage and then discuss division of property as the next logical step.

Crouch says that marriage is the only contract that anyone can break, at any time, and not be held responsible for it.

> "So getting married in America is like doing business in Russia. Everything is up for grabs, everything is constantly renegotiated, and nobody has to keep their word. I think that makes for a lot of unhappy marriages."[1]

The Dollar Costs of Divorce

From a cost perspective, divorce can be economically damaging not only for the state but also for couples. Consider these figures:

⇨ US divorces cost the country $33 billion annually or $312.00 per household;

⇨ The average divorce in America costs state and federal governments $30,000 in direct and indirect costs. Direct costs to the state include child support enforcement, Medicaid payments, temporary assistance to needy families fund (TANF), food stamps and public housing assistance.[2]

---

[1] John Crouch, Executive Director. Americans for Divorce Reform, Arlington, Virginia. www.divorceform@usa.net.
[2] David G. Schramm, Utah State University, USA.

⇨ To the couple, divorce costs about $18,000 and this would include lost work productivity, relocation costs and legal fees that vary immensely, depending on the nature of the divorce and the situation of the couple.[3]

The Emotional Costs of Divorce

And what about the argument that divorce makes people happier after they leave a sad marriage?

Studies appear to suggest that this is a myth, because evidence points to the contrary. According to the Institute of American Values, when divorced couples were rated with couples who stayed married on 12 parameters of psychological well-being, it was discovered that on average, couples who divorced were no happier five years after the divorce than were equally unhappily married couples who stayed together.[4]

---

[3] David G. Schramm
[4] Katherine Heine, Cox News Service, Nov. 2005 (www.americanvalues.org/html/r-unhappy_ii.html)

There are other reasons why divorced individuals don't end up happier:

- Depression symptoms do not necessarily diminish with divorce, nor did divorce raise people's self-esteem;

- Unhappy marriages were less common than unhappy spouses;
- Staying married did not typically trap unhappy spouses in violent relationships.[5]

Ms. Heines also raised the litigation aspect in most divorces. She said that a significant number of married people usually want to settle their divorce with the least possible hassle, but divorce lawyers are a species to be reckoned with. They come up with arguments to justify getting into World War III, and they drag out the paper work.

For divorcing couples who become emotionally and financially spent, is the courtroom drama really all that worth it? Couldn't couples just talk about their differences without third parties who are in it to line their pockets?

---

[5] Katherine Heine.

Painless Divorce?

Many lawyers, and those who care to admit it, agree: a painless divorce, like painless dentistry, is non-existent. And the trauma – legal or emotional – continues to be felt long after divorcing couples have left the courts.

Explaining why divorce costs time, energy and money, a lawyer from the law offices of E. Carroll Strauss had this to say:

> "And whether we notice it or not... marriage is way more like "Joe and Wilma, Inc." than "happily ever after." When we say "I do" we then enter into an economic partnership. We buy cars, houses, books, big-screen TVs. We make babies. We make plans. We make assumptions. We get disappointed...Like shareholders, we have invested in the partnership. We invest time, we invest money and we invest emotions. We invest all of

these in hopes, and we invest all these things in dreams, and we invest all of these in security. Rare is the man or woman who can walk away from these investments... so de-investing is painful."

Divorce and Children

A specialist in human development and family studies from the University of Missouri discussed the impact of divorce on children, mentioning that how they react strongly and differently to their divorcing parents depends on their age.

⇨ Infants: higher degree of irritability, more crying and fussing, changes in sleeping and eating habits.

⇨ Toddlers: they recognize the fact that one parent is no longer living at home, they have a difficult time physically separating from a parent, may express anger, may lose some skills previously acquired like toilet training, going back to thumb-sucking, experience changes in sleeping patterns, may have nightmares.

⇨ <u>Pre-schoolers and early elementary age</u>: may blame themselves for the divorce, may over-worry about changes in their lives, may exhibit sadness and grieving because of the absence of one parent, may be aggressive and violent to the parent they blame for the divorce, may fantasize about their parents getting back together.

⇨ <u>Pre-teens:</u> may feel abandoned by the departing parent, may withdraw from friends and favourite activities, may exhibit strange behaviour and use foul language, may feel angry and uncertain about their concepts of love, marriage and family, may feel that they are growing up too soon, and may find themselves preoccupied about their parents' finances.

Some Eye-Opening Statistics

➢ Although divorced people may have successful subsequent marriages, the divorce rate of remarriages is actually higher than that of first marriages,

➢ Those who get into a live-in arrangement before marrying have a considerably higher chance of divorcing. Reasons are not that clear. This can probably be explained by the fact that the type of people who tend to co-habit may also be those who are more willing to divorce. There is proof that supports the notion that cohabitation itself generates attitudes in people that are more conducive to divorce, one example of which is the thinking that living together is temporary, and hence an arrangement that can easily be terminated.

➢ Qualitative studies and long term empirical studies have demonstrated that children develop interpersonal problems that become worse in adulthood, thus affecting their own chances at a happy marriage.

➤ As inferred from the previous statement, children of divorce have a much higher rate of divorce than children whose parents stayed together. The old adage that parents set the example is true in this case. Children learn about commitment and permanence from parents. For children of divorced parents, these concepts have already been undermined or shaken.

➢ No marriage is perfect. Using a large sample for research purposes, researchers learned that 86 percent of people who were unhappily married in the late 1980s, but stayed with the marriage, indicated that, when interviewed five years later, they were happier. In fact 3/5 of those who were previously unhappy considered their marriages as either "very happy" or "quite happy."[6]

➢ A marriage counsellor, after counselling hundreds of couples who were on the path to divorce, raised the idea of "self-talk" as one potential cause of divorce. This pattern of negative self talk, he contends, is a barrier to a couple's happiness, much more than a lack of open communication is.

Self talk is the equivalent of an individual's thoughts. He said:

---

[6] David Popenoe, the National Marriage Project at Rutgers University, New Brunswick, N.J, 2002.

"Most people do not control their thoughts (self-talk), but they allow their thoughts to control them...for instance, if a man speaks negatively to himself about his wife and he permits this self-talk, he will attract a host of other negative thoughts. As a result of these negative thoughts, he will experience negative feelings – anger, jealousy, fear, even hatred, and these negative thoughts and feelings will lead to actions that tend to break up the relationship."[7]

The previous statement above clues us into one of the deep-seated causes of divorce, and how this can be easily solved, if couples were honest with themselves and with each other. Sometimes, it's not so much the lack of communication that leads to the breakdown (for after all, aren't men less talkative and less spontaneous than women?), but the pattern of negative thinking that each spouse continually nurtures.

---

[7] Dr. H.B. Biem, Separate Future. Centax Books. Saskatchewan, Canada. 1993.

It is surprising to learn how often trivial the reasons are for divorcing, because their personal frustrations and unresolved personal issues are often blown out of proportion.

The Case for Staying Married (It's still the best institution there is!)

It all comes down to attitude, doesn't it? Cynics have called marriage the "old ball and chain." Many happily married individuals disagree, because they don't see marriage as slavery and bondage, where one's natural instincts and desires have to play second fiddle to the happiness of the other half.

Happily married couples say that marriage has taught them to accept each other's strengths and possibilities. They argue that by doing that, they transform themselves from the ordinary to the extraordinary.

Marriage therefore is an "enabling" form of situation where it means the freedom to be who they really are, to reach for the stars and discover what they are meant to be without ridicule or rejection.

Marriage and Happiness

Many of us have read reports that drive home the message: married people are healthier and happier, and hence live longer than single or celibate individuals.

For one, there is the emotional support they receive when the going gets rough, and the fact that married life provides the opportunities to sustain communication between two people, even if one of the spouses just wants to vent out. In fact one of the reasons people say they like being married is the assurance that there is someone they can come home to at the end of a hard day.

For Better or For Worse...

"For better or for worse" is still very much a strong argument for getting – and staying – married. While some people would be too shy to admit it, the love and support in times of illness can speed up recovery.

People in fact like the "for better or for worse" aspect of marriage because it tells them that no matter what happens, someone will be around.

It goes beyond having a security or safety net. It's the knowledge that they can count on someone when times are bad, and that alone generates a considerable degree of peace of mind and a sense of calm for the soul.

And here's a romantic – but true - notion of marriage, to which happily married couples will agree: "Marriage moves us from ego to we-go.

The single self shifts from me first to the sacred union of *us*...values such as love, honesty, respect, fidelity and dependability form the engine of a good marriage. Little kindnesses are the oil. Without the oil, it will grind. With it, it glides."[8]

And how about the simplest reasons for marriage such as: silly little jokes, hugs and cuddling, traveling together, laughing together, quiet times together, mutual friends, sexual intimacy, pillow talk, kissing and making up? Can anyone really put a price tag on these simple pleasures? Don't they echo the saying that the best things in life are free?

Oh yes, there is love in relationships, but there is deeper love in a marriage that is on its way to its 25th or 50th year. Sir Arthur Wing Pinero sums it nicely: "those who love deeply never grow old; they may die of old age, but they die young." So did James Thurber: "A lady of 47 who has been married 27 years and has six children knows what love really is and once described it to me like this: *love is what you've been through with somebody*.

---

[8] Paula Dore of Glenview, Illinois, who participated in the National Marriage Encounter, an initiative that is all over the United States as compiled by Michael Leach and Therese J. Borchard (editors). I Like Being Married. Doubleday Books. New York. 2002.

People who have remained happily married are those who realize gradually that there are actually two marriage contracts, not just one.

The first contract is what everyone is familiar with – the one that the priest in a wedding ceremony makes official. The second contract is what couples call the silent contract. It is secret, implicit and largely unconscious. It is this second contract that specifies standards and behaviours our partner should fulfill.

The distinguishing characteristic of this contract is our secret belief that our own feelings, needs, and sense of what is right are most important. One's expectations of the other can carry risks and can lead to clashes, which couples try to resolve among themselves.

Unfortunately, as mentioned earlier, these conversations are rarely objective or fruitful, given that individuals rarely ask if their expectations are fair and reasonable – they just complain endlessly. Happily married couples are those who understand this second silent contract and all of its ramifications.[9]

---

[9] Doctors Melvyn Kinder and Connell Cowan. Husbands and Wives: Exploding Marital Myths, Deepening Love and Desire. Clarkson N Potter Inc., New York. 1989.

Happily married couples are those who continue to invest in the marriage, knowing that for love to flourish, it takes hard work and substantial amounts of creativity.

Love and physical attraction may take the backseat, especially when the children arrive, but fulfilled couples know that they must stick it out, through thick and thin, for the sake of the emotional well-being of the children.

When couples think of others and not just themselves and make a continuing effort to make the marriage work, they've made the best investment they could ever make and they firmly believe in this.

The need to make the partnership work is often the secret of happy marriages. As Masters and Johnson said, "Although these marriages may be loveless, they are not necessarily bad. Even good marriages are susceptible to a disappearance of love."[10]

---

[10] William Masters, Virginia Johnson, Robert Kolodny. Masters and Johnson on Sex and Human Loving. Little, Brown & Company, Ltd. USA. 1985.

Marriage and Instinct

Dr. Mary Pipher, a therapist and anthropologist, points to the family as still an essential unit of the community. When people get married, their hopes are linked to building a home and family.

Dr. Pipher maintains that families are ancient institutions. She said that ever since humans crossed the savannas in search of food, our families have been unique...Homo sapiens needs families to survive, and bravo to those millions of parents who are trying hard to do the right thing.

Happily married people understand this very basic concept. It is not just their own nucleus that needs caring, but the entire institution of marriage and the social unit known as a family.

When marriages flourish, so do families, and as a result, communities all over the world also flourish. That is how societies become stronger and progressive. When the smallest unit survives, the larger ones survive.

"I write about families because I love them. When I travel alone far from home, I think of my children's faces to calm myself down. I picture them smiling, studying, playing violin or volleyball. I picture my husband's face bent over his guitar or relaxed and fresh, the way it is on the mornings when we drink coffee together on the front porch. Those faces are my mandalas. They comfort and secure me. The faces of those we love are the first, the primal, mandalas for us all."[11]

These are the sentiments that happily married people nurture and sustain in their hearts. If they focused on their mandalas instead of on their frustrations and unfulfilled desires, these are the people who have shown an incredible willingness of reaching out, of seeing past their own egos.

(Marriage is not the extension of the romance junkie phase. It is equivalent to a long term commitment that emotionally intelligent husbands and wives understand fully.

[11] Doctor Mary Pipher. The Shelter of Each Other: Rebuilding our Families. G.P. Putnam's Sons, New York. 1996.

They know, deep in their hearts, that love and passion will not always be on the daily agenda, and may diminish as the responsibilities of their marriage take them to the next level – family life.

To conclude this section, here is a statement extracted from the book, *Anatomy of Love* by Helen E. Fisher:

"When Darwin used the term **survival of the fittest,** he was not referring to your good looks or your bank account; he was counting your children. If you raise babies that have babies, you are what nature calls fit. You have passed your genes to the next generation and in terms of survival you have won…only in tandem can either men or women reproduce and pass on the beat of life."

How to Save Your Marriage

We have painted the unpleasant side of divorce to help you realize that it may not necessarily be the solution to your unhappiness, and in the second section, we've advanced arguments to promote the numerous advantages of marriage and staying married.

But life does have hitches and will always be full of obstacles, threatening the stability of married life. We now offer some tips on how to save your marriage when you sense that it's on the rocks or needs a re-overhauling.

Recognizing Gender Differences

Men and women perceive emotion, communication, sex, fidelity, work and money because of the way they were socialized and because they have been shaped by their own parents' perceptions.

They bring these ideas into the marriage and hence have their own baggage of beliefs regarding what is tolerable and intolerable in a marriage, what they have to give their spouse and what to expect in return.

Writing the book, "*For Better or For Worse*", Heatherington and Kelly illustrate this point more clearly when they mention the different ways men and women choose a partner:

"Women approach love as informed consumers…they kick the tires, look under the hood, run the motor, check the mileage. Women love love, but being practical-minded, not enough to ignore potential defects. Good looks and romantic love matter to a woman, but in considering potential suitors, a woman also looks at the practical, such as a suitor's economic prospects, emotional stability, trustworthiness, and what kind of father he will be…Despite a reputation for practicality, males come off as hopeless romantics. They are much more prone to fall head-over-heels in love…and also more prone to idealize the object of their affection. If the bodywork is good and the grille pretty,

> often a man will buy on the spot, no questions asked."[12]

It takes practice to learn that gender differences do not constitute threats to a marriage, but a cause for celebration and an opportunity to expand an individual's sphere of experience.

Try to remember that your partner is not your mirror image. In a loving, effective partnership, individuality and separateness are wholesome concepts that each spouse must work at.

A Word from the Cos!

Bill Cosby, the famous American comedian and still married to the same woman, said that these gender differences – that women are not just men who can have babies and men

---

[12] E. Mavis Heatherington and John Kelly. For Better or for Worse. W.W. Norton & Company, New York, 2002.

are not just women who spike footballs – give marriage its vitality, its dynamics and its delights…He says, "Americans may like the style called unisex, but the wiser French have a devout appreciation of the wonder they call *la difference.*"

A true understanding of these gender differences should therefore lead us to the proper notion of a marriage. While many people view marriage as a fusion, making two separate individuals one, we must still keep our own personality and deal with our own problems ourselves.

> "Marriage is ultimately about two relatively whole individuals coming together to create a union that can be even greater than the sum of the parts. But each of us must always be aware that a lack of self-confidence is own separate job to fix. We can look to our mate for support, but not for magical solutions."[13]

---

[13] Kinder and Cowan, Husbands and Wives (footnote 9)

Notice the Small Stuff

"Don't sweat the small stuff" is probably one advice that does not always work for marriage, because it is important to notice the small stuff, if the marriage were to flourish. Steve Carter cites an important fact about relationships: most of the real work in relationships is taking place in **quieter** moments in **smaller** spaces.

Examples would be:

➢ avoiding bringing up the defective garage door while your husband is rushing to meet a deadline and needs to focus on his project for a few hours;

➢ attending to the kids and keeping them away from the kitchen while your wife prepares dinner;

➢ offering to pick up your husband's shirts at the dry cleaner's because he forgot to do it yesterday;

➢ filling up the car tank if you know that your husband has to drive out of town on a client visit;

➢ taking your wife dancing because she's always loved to dance even if you have two left feet and have always hated it.

And What of Money?

One irritant in a marriage is money.

Chances are spouses have their own ways of spending and saving money. If both husband and wife earn similar salaries, agree on how to split the house expenses prior to getting married so no one feels cheated or disadvantaged financially.

While it was fine to expect him to pay for dinner and the movie while you were dating, marriage calls for a genuine economic partnership.

Or, if you know that your husband is particularly averse to useless shopping sprees, make an effort to reduce your shopping trips and concentrate on the essentials instead of on your whims. Don't forget to discuss your investment preferences and try to stick to a budget and a savings plan.

And What of Politics?

The same is true for sex and politics: if your husband likes to watch a pornographic films as a prelude to love making, let him know that you're not particularly in favour of this practice but do indulge him occasionally. If your wife likes to visit synagogue and do charity work in her parish, don't express any resentment or complain that she's spending too much time on her fund-raising activities.

Work on keeping your partner stimulated intellectually. If there's anything that grates, it's a wife who constantly talks about what's on sale and a husband who knows nothing but what teams made it to the NFL playoffs this year.

Look back to courtship days when both of you could talk until the wee hours of the morning because you were interested in what each of you did in the office that day, in that bookseller or movie, or how the Dow Jones sparkled because of news about Intel or Microsoft, etc.

Enrich each other with your experiences and vicarious experiences. Let the other know that you have an interest in life and what it has to offer, and make every effort not to be a boring mate by reading more, experimenting more, and living more.

Alone Time

Many people say that children put a damper on the marriage. Who has time for love and passion when the kids are screaming their lungs off or running a 105 degree fever? Or when money has to be scrounged for to pay for those expensive braces?

Raising children can turn us into impatient, stressed-out beings so if hiring a baby sitter overnight will not disrupt the monthly budget, do so and go away – just the two of you.

But don't use that time away from children to complain about each other's habits or to raise past incidents!

Instead of looking at marriage blessed with high points or fraught with low points, think of it instead as a series of turning points.

Turning Points

Dr. Sonya Rhodes says these turning points must be regarded as opportunities to make a marriage stronger and more fulfilling.

These turning points become crystal clear at mid-life where couples have developed a keener sense of time limitations and an urgency in their desire to make the most out of their marriage and their lives.

The mid-life years are a natural time for reflections: couples now have the advantage of being able to see where they have been, where they are and where they want to go. When a 46-year old woman came to see Dr. Rhodes in an effort to save her marriage, she said, "This might be my last chance to make things better. I don't want last chances to become lost chances."[14]

Complimenting and Praising

Give credit where it's due, be generous with compliments and be sincere in your praise. Do you sometimes find yourself wishing that your partner would compliment you the way your boss does after a job well done?

Many couples discover that as they settle into their marriage, the compliments or kind praises are not as frequent as when they were dating.

---

[14] Dr. Sonya Rhodes. Second Honeymoon. A Pioneering Guide for Reviving the Mid-Life Marriage. William Morrow & Co., New York, 1992.

Making it a practice to give credit where it's due and being sincere about your praises go a long way towards reinforcing wellness in a marriage.

If you see that your wife works conscientiously on the treadmill to keep off the weight, did you ever think that she's probably doing this to please you? Saying something like, "You're so disciplined in your efforts to achieve your goals, I'm proud of you" will add to her self-confidence and reinforce her attitude that she's doing something that's healthy and that you appreciate.

If your husband is good at crunching numbers, praise him for his skills at rapid calculation. "You're amazing with numbers" will give him a sense of pride, and he will feel important to you.

No doubt many experts and marriage counselors will differ in opinion on how to save a marriage, but they all agree on the following fundamental elements of a solid marriage – only the words and the way they are conveyed are different:

- ✓ trust and communication

- ✓ respect for each other's ideas and expectations
- ✓ fidelity

- ✓ physical and intellectual stimulation

- ✓ maintaining their own personalities, but supporting each other's dreams

The Concept of Friendship in Marriage

Friends are forever. Even if we move out of town or take up residence overseas, we maintain our friendships.

We certainly don't divorce our friends just because of a misunderstanding, so if we treated our spouse as a dear friend, we probably won't ever need a divorce lawyer and go through the painful exercise of property division – a course of action that can spell financial ruin for many.

Since love is less permanent (we fall in and out of love a few times in our lifetime) and friendship more durable, every attempt must be made to make our spouse not only a lover and a partner, but also a friend.

Friendship is evident manifestation of maturity. Marriage is a responsibility larger than life, and can be a source of annoyance or profound joy. Only when we turn those annoyances and joys into building blocks for an enduring friendship can we say that we've taken the unwavering path to a marriage made in heaven.

Friendship is EVERYTHING!

If there is true friendship between husband and wife, the marriage avoids landing on the rocks. Instead it becomes a rock-hard marriage where no individual or circumstance can put it asunder.

In fact, it is the genuine friendship between two people that put more meaning in the words, "for richer or for poorer, for better or for worse, till death do us part" - what Mary Pipher calls "the shelter of each other."

Friendship in a marriage means that the marriage will be pregnant with memories of laughter and humour, for didn't we choose those friends who made us laugh the most? Didn't our mothers always tell us, "when choosing a husband, count the times he made you laugh."

Friendship also means open and honest communication; a no holds barred type of union where our comfort level with our spouse goes beyond 100%, assured that what we say and how we say it will not be judged or taken in a negative light.

If you talk to married people, a wish they frequently express is that they remain the best of friends and the closest of companions. Surveys in fact reveal that if there is one component that will enable a couple to weather the tough times, it is friendship.

As a famous poet once said, "No man is an island." Kinder and Cowan agree that friendship is the antidote to loneliness. Getting married does not mean that people will never experience loneliness, "but it does diminish our sense of separateness."

Friendship between couples generates wholesome feelings of goodwill and fidelity. Our spouse – our friend – has our interests at heart, will not betray us and will be our staunchest supporter. Friendship also makes spouses stronger; this strength is reinforced by the joy of shared history, of nostalgia and plans for the future.

Romance is a good thing, and we could use heaps of it when our relationships get rocky. But mature friends are aware that romance can be a barrier to friendship. Why? Because romance obliterates the darker side of our existence – our fears, anxieties, and insecurities. Yet, it is those fears, anxieties and insecurities that naturally draw us to our friend.

Friendship in a marriage brings about the recognition that flux, de-stabilization and disruption are what Dr. Rhodes calls the "first steps in the dynamic process of repair, rebuilding and renewal."[15]

---

[15] Dr. Sonya Rhodes, ibid.

Familiarity does NOT breed contempt. It breeds content. A sense of contentment equates with satisfaction, warmth, and unwavering assurance. Sharing a life together in love and friendship makes for a book that is deeper and thicker in shared histories, in content.

If you were to ask a happy bachelor and a happily married man to each write their stories, you'd get a positive narration from both. The single person's perspective would however be I, me and myself – and possibly a string of blind dates and Saturday nights alone. The married man will talk about "us", of mutual interests – a story definitely made richer because there are two stories, not one.

Conclusion

We like to be judged in terms of what we have accomplished in the human relationships department. Read this statement:

> "I managed to get my client half of her husband's properties overseas and alimony and child support payments of close to $250,000 a year plus the three cars, the country home, his art collection and half of his stocks."

Compare the foregoing with this one:

> "I didn't really do anything special that I can be proud of, except perhaps provide adequately for my family and raise good children. Happily, they turned out to be well-abiding citizens and I guess that's the best reward there is."

In the first statement, we see shades of greed and materialism, in the second, humility and self-effacement. Who has made a genuine contribution for the betterment of society?

Much as it sounds terribly old-fashioned, marriage is a commitment, and individuals must make every attempt not to cheapen that commitment in any way. Staying married is a lifelong, missionary-like endeavour.

It takes guts. It takes nerves of steel to make a marriage work. A sense of humour and a lower degree of self-importance can sustain us in that work.

The obstacles will be numerous, and there will be situations where we will question our sanity, unsure if we can really hang in there.

It will be a monumental effort to remain attracted to the same qualities that attracted you to your spouse on the first day you met. Your spouse is still the same person you fell in love with, he has not changed his soul, his being, only his wardrobe.

So if there's only way to divorce, but a thousand ways to save your marriage, which path will you choose? Are you going to throw in the towel or take up one more challenge?

There's very little meaning to saving face or saving dollars; it's much more noble and enduring to save souls. But you won't unlock the meaning of this statement in your youth or in your 30's.

Best to wait until you reach mid-life, until your maturity has come full circle, and you get to the point where you don't want to turn your back on the most important investment of your life, where every nerve of your body cries out, "You've got to save us."

Appendix

An extract from Bill Cosby's book, Love and Marriage. Doubleday Books, New York. 1989.

Therefore, in spite of what Thomas Jefferson wrote, all men may be created equal, but not to all women, and the loveliest love affair must bear the strain of this inequality once the ceremony is over. When a husband and wife settle down together, there is a natural struggle for power...and in this struggle, the husband cannot avoid giving up a few things – for example dinner.

To be fair, I must admit that Camille did wait a few years before allowing me to make this particular sacrifice. I had just sat down at the table one night with her and our three children when I happened to notice that my plate contained only collard greens and brown rice.

"Would you please donate this to the Hare Krishna and bring me my real meal," I said to the gentleman serving the food.

"You have it all," he replied.

"No, what I have is a snack for the North Korean Army. The meat must have slipped off somewhere. Why don't we try to find it together?"

"Mrs. Cosby said we are no longer eating meat."

"She did?" I looked down the table at Camille. "Dear, if I got a letter from the Pope, do you think I could..."

"Bill, meat is bad for us and we just have to cut it out. It's full of fat that could kill you. I'm sorry, I forgot to tell you."

"So am I. I could've started eating out at a place where they don't mind who they kill."

"Honey, lots of people are vegetarians."

"And lots of people like to get hit with whips, but I've managed to be happy not joining them."

Nevertheless I became a vegetarian. A husband should go with the flow of his marriage, even when that flow leads over a cliff.

About two years later, however, I sat down to dinner one night and a steak suddenly appeared on my plate.

"Look at this," I said to the gentleman serving the food. "Someone has lost a steak. Would you please return it to its owner?"

"Mrs. Cosby said we are eating meat again," he told me.

"How nice to see the cows come home," I said.

References:

John Crouch, Executive Director. Americans for Divorce Reform, Arlington, Virginia. www.divorceform@usa.net.

David G. Schramm, Utah State University, USA.

Katherine Heine, Cox News Service, Nov. 2005 (www.americanvalues.org/html/r-unhappy_ii.html)

David Popenoe, the National Marriage Project at Rutgers University, New Brunswick, N.J, 2002.

Dr. H.B. Biem, Separate Future. Centax Books. Saskatchewan, Canada. 1993.

Paula Dore of Glenview, Illinois, who participated in the National Marriage Encounter, an initiative that is all over the United States as compiled by Michael Leach and Therese J. Borchard (editors). I Like Being Married. Doubleday Books. New York. 2002.

Doctors Melvyn Kinder and Connell Cowan. Husbands and Wives: Exploding Marital Myths, Deepening Love and Desire. Clarkson N Potter Inc., New York. 1989.

William Masters, Virginia Johnson, Robert Kolodny. Masters and Johnson on Sex and Human Loving. Little, Brown & Company, Ltd. USA. 1985.

Doctor Mary Pipher. The Shelter of Each Other: Rebuilding our Families. G.P. Putnam's Sons, New York. 1996.

E. Mavis Heatherington and John Kelly. For Better or for Worse. W.W. Norton & Company, New York, 2002.

Dr. Sonya Rhodes. Second Honeymoon. A Pioneering Guide for Reviving the Mid-Life Marriage. William Morrow & Co., New York, 1992.